BOA

EDITIONS LTD

The Second O ot Sorrow

POEMS

SEAN THOMAS DOUGHERTY

American Poets Continuum Series, No. 165

BOA Editions, Ltd. ❧ Rochester, NY ❧ 2018

First Edition
18 19 20 21 7 6 5 4 3 2 1

For information about permission to reuse any material from this book, please
contact The Permissions Company at www.permissionscompany.com or e-mail
permdude@gmail.com.

Publications by BOA Editions, Ltd.—a not-for-profit corporation
under section 501 (c) (3) of the United States Internal Revenue
Code—are made possible with funds from a variety of sources,
including public funds from the Literature Program of the
National Endowment for the Arts; the New York State Council
on the Arts, a state agency; and the County of Monroe, NY.
Private funding sources include the Lannan Foundation for
support of the Lannan Translations Selection Series; the Max
and Marian Farash Charitable Foundation; the Mary S. Mulligan
Charitable Trust; the Rochester Area Community Foundation; the Steeple-
Jack Fund; the Ames-Amzalak Memorial Trust in memory of Henry Ames,
Semon Amzalak, and Dan Amzalak; and contributions from many individuals
nationwide. See Colophon on page 72 for special individual acknowledgments.

ART WORKS.
arts.gov

State of the Arts

NYSCA

Cover Design: Sandy Knight
Cover Art: "Motel Peninsula" by Greg Valiga
Interior Design and Composition: Richard Foerster
Manufacturing: McNaughton & Gunn
BOA Logo: Mirko

Library of Congress Cataloging-in-Publication Data

Names: Dougherty, Sean Thomas, author.
Title: The second O of sorrow / Sean Thomas Dougherty.
Description: First edition. | Rochester, NY : BOA Editions, Ltd., [2018] |
  Series: American reader series ; no. 165
Identifiers: LCCN 2017045511 | ISBN 9781942683551 (softcover : acid-free
  paper)
Classification: LCC PS3554.O8213 A6 2018 | DDC 811/.54--dc23 LC record
available at https://lccn.loc.gov/2017045511

BOA Editions, Ltd.
250 North Goodman Street, Suite 306
Rochester, NY 14607
www.boaeditions.org
A. Poulin, Jr., Founder (1938–1996)

Contents

The Second O of Sorrow

"Forgive me if this seems
extreme—I don't know how to make things
ordinary anymore, though I dress and go to work
each day as if the world were ordinary . . ."
　　　—Susan Aizenberg

"What keeps us awake,
other than the clock's sweeping hand
moving like a slow-cresting wave,
is the sound of no sound, the sound
of drifting, of grieving, of not letting go,
of trying to find a name for this."
　　　—January Gill O'Neil

"Apollinaire lived in Paris, I live in Cleveland, Ohio."
　　　—Hart Crane

"I'll love you like I love you
Then I'll die"
　　　—Land of Talk

Why Bother?

Because right now, there is   someone

out there with

a wound   in the exact shape

                                     of your words.

The Second O of Sorrow

Somehow, I am still here, long after
transistor radios, the eight-tracks my father blared

driving from town to town across Ohio
selling things, the music where we danced

just to keep alive. I now understand I was not
supposed to leave so soon, half a century

a kind of boulder that I've pushed up the hill
& now for a moment, like Sisyphus

I watch it roll.
I walk through the snow.

I breathe the dirty East Side wind
pushing past the Russian church, the scent

of fish & freighters & the refinery
filling the hole in my chest—how many years

have piled since I last stumbled out onto the ice
& sat down to die.

Only to look up at the geometry
of sky—& stood

to face whoever might need me—

What Do You Say to a Daughter When She Suspects Her Mother Is Dying

That feverish perfume of the wound on her mother's foot is the songbird of the bees, the xylophone of her bent spine is making a cacophonous chatter, that there is a silence to the stars we may once return to. That she should go outside and play. Write your name on the stoop. Make a drawing of a house that flies through the sky. You hunt around for chalk. You concentrate on the colors like fuchsia and magenta that conceal a dark brightness. Draw with me a window in the sidewalk you say. Where are we going she asks? You want to tell her a new hospital, a new doctor with tools like in *Star Trek* that they scan over her mother's body and heal her wounds, her blood, her veins. Or back to a place and a time where the Medicine Mother grinds a few twigs, some leaves into a powder that tells the body again how to spell the names of the Gods in its bones. You want to say draw me a window so I may step into and take you to see her when you were a baby and she could run through the grass through the Balkan fields of yellow flowers and climb the mountain of the cross. A window to show her before her mother's hands turned blue as the sky after it has snowed.

My Grief Grows a White Flower

Tonight, it is my grief who speaks
beneath the dying laurel tree

in late bloom, this spring evening.
Silence is its rotting womb

eaten from the inside by red ants,
the hole in the black center

of its trunk, my daughters cannot
climb or its limbs will break,

the one your father planted
when you were first born,

now like you it bends
in the coming storm, the clouds

that push across the slate sky.
Nothing stills its weeping,

nothing is hushed, the branches
sway a slow dirge, & Death,

who has become my companion,
I hear beneath the wailing wind

the quiet click of his bony fingers
weaves a wreath of fallen thorns.

After Surgery

Forget the red berries on the snow. Forget how you were hungry but couldn't eat, and the nurse who never came soon enough with the morphine. Forget the pain. Your pale face like a small moon. Your hair unwashed and unbraided, and all the papers they made us sign like citations. And the long walk from the parking lot in the snow, nervous I would not see you again, as I drove our daughters to school then rushing back across town to hold your IV'd arm. To wipe the drool from your mouth. And then more doctors, and the veins they couldn't find. The holes they left in your arms. And the tests that told us nothing. And then another surgery, and another, and another, then it was time to go home, because we had one. With lists of appointments like citations, your limbs bandaged and bruised. Before we left, I glanced out that seventh-story window, down at the street of strangers rushing off to the normal world we no longer belonged to—

In the Light of One Lamp

I crawled into bed and closed my eyes and not long after heard the small hooves of the horses, the tiny ones that gallop in our dreams, or are they the dreams of our children, galloping through the black ruins. Everything we do is against the crippling light. To hear them cry at night is to know they are alive. When they are scared they come galloping down the long hall calling your name. Tonight, it is our oldest daughter, the red mare with her fiery mane, she snuggles in between us and falls back to sleep in your arms, to that secret place inside her, she barely moves, crossing over the river, through a grove of alders, through the black ruins, she is the one who once whispered, *the grass it knows everything.*

The Bravery of Birds

My daughters are shouting at the starlings in their murmuration. Their mother watches from a porch chair. The writhing pain, as if she is a broken necklace. Stones of pearls in the grass. Even the oxy does not help. The light of pills. The color of nausea. The color of sunlight for the crippled and the lame? To get up each day despite hopelessness. I think of Bernadette, and how they questioned her, the brilliant light of Mary who appeared to her in a grotto and offered water to heal the world. They called her a liar and a cheat. And only after decades was it revealed: the tumors and the pain that ravaged Bernadette. You will not be happy in this world, the Mother of God explained. And yet in the scrubbing of floors, the life lived in a cell away from the world, in this suffering there must have been something more. We go on suffering without fear? Though Bernadette suffered, was there envy or fear? Was there joy? Who of us is ever not weary? I watch the starlings swoop and dive as if they know the air will never let them go. My daughters run and their mother rocks in her chair and holds her bandaged foot, and bites down hard against the pain. And I want to ask her if she ever returns to that room overlooking the bay, when she was strong. And the lavender was high. And a few green flies buzzed against the screen. And the scent of salt and sea roses wafted through the window we left open, lying naked on the bed in the amethyst-colored light. O Love, were we too not afraid?

Scribbled on the Scaffolding of

You can love someone fiercely. You can love them like a country. You can love them like a cathedral, or like a fretting child. And then they leave you. Even if they are right there, they go somewhere else. You tell them come back and they turn towards the gutter's wind. They cook casseroles. You start to put a brick down in your chest. Then another brick. And that wall grows. You get going. And the waters rise behind that giant wall. You can say you get no more of my heart. You can move on. You can tell them to their face. You can drive a thousand miles. You can drive a thousand more. Years can pass. And then one day you look up and you can find in their face that person you loved from years ago. And it all goes to hell, that Giant Dam you built crumbles and falls, and it all floods out, and you dive straight down and deep as you can in that long-lost drowning. Let them find my body floating on that river. Let them say he dived deeper than anyone. Let them carry me to her and lay me at her feet. Then pour the gasoline. And strike the match and the plumes of ash will flutter all around my Beloved's hands like black butterflies.

We a New Ledger

I want to find a new name for the wind, for the smoke
curling around her eyes in some punk club
after hours high. I want to rewrite each day after it dies,
so it may keep us breathing. The barbiturates of our mouths.
Push into the black dirt, lying in the long grass
outside of an abandoned farm house,
the soft cindered earth of our dead.
I want to find one new word for making music,
a language which is nearly song itself,
electric as copper tubing joining our palms
into applause, or more like the pause
right before the clapping, the rising hairs
on the back of our hands. Where is the name for that?
A name like a birthmark in a small town to get some fix.
What is the smeared name written inside a matchbook?
The strange scratching on the wooden pallet at work,
the letters you can read in the seeded grass, the shape
of a clipped fingernail is a moon and a word.
How nearly everything was. A name to disown
what has been done. A new name for the rain,
a new name for a cloud, an old name for the dirt.
The oldest we witness. Gripping it in our two fists.

Poem Written with a Cough

After we were fired from the hospital
    we dove into Prince.

We shot junk & ate junk food
    & watched MTV for weeks.

We fucked on the bare mattress
    with our futures now behind us.

The lengthening of our shadows
    ground down my teeth.

All the noise was brilliant, a radio
    in my brain I tuned to the station

I hummed the beautiful static of tiny pills.
    I peeled the torn red wallpaper

& wrote my dairy of the amber rain
    on the scraps. Outside, a fire escape

that led to an alley.
    I'd climb down to stare at the brick wall.

I folded my body into an envelope
    & mailed it to the department of dead letters.

~

Stories are seeds & the circus
    of us was like a trapeze

of sunflowers, bowing
    in the deserted lot of decades

beside the closed
        down paper mill—

maybe the dope man wouldn't arrive—
        for you the matchstick girl

by the side of the road.
        I refused to betray

like the small wooden figurine
        of the Black Madonna you clutched

in your coat pocket. Luck
        in little ways, you always said.

To protect us—
        like the glint of a blade.

We used to cut the cord.
        When you kissed you tasted

like peppermints
        you stole from the bowl

of every clinic counter.
        You my crushed orchid—

How we trembled
        like the lighter's flame

to the bent spoon

of our bodies—

We Pay the Rent We Breathe

To say the word orange
is to say a kind of light,

the light of our daughter,
as she peels an orange

at the hospital, beside your IV'd arm
already beginning to infiltrate,

every day the pills
you were—
we were our own exile

on the bare mattress,
our daughter's chord

diminished,
down the dark hallway
towards her crib, your swayed

reaching—
removed the night's sleep mask.

Across the arm's frets, the small prick

& then the push; leaning
in the pool hall door,

another one of your ex's boys
strung-out, swallowed

peace by jagged piece.
In the city of stray dogs

& stolen cell phones,
the pregnant girl

at the Get Go Mart
with the quart of liquor

& a box of menthols.

Grief

I nodded into the wet dog smell of it
heaved it over my back,

carried it like a man
who bears a wooden cross,

he will nail himself to—

Triptych of Desire and the Duende

The wind had been sitting for some time.
I dreamed I was a porter in a house of fog.
Someone was sandpapering a chair.
Desire: Let's take a sabbatical from the burning edges.
I need a new coat. One they wore before I was born.
At the intersection of Imagination and Death, the Kids of Chance
    drive past their own tombs.
High on glass.
And lyrics of astonishing levies.
Month after month, year after year.
To reassemble the eyes, out of this appalling place.
The gaunt priests of the street corner calling their price.
Gun shots and guitars.
And who chanted, tenderness resembles a quiet river. Desire is the
    flood.
The choreography of the trees.
Every time we kiss we are saying goodbye.
There is nothing I want to tell you except through the dark.
What does it all matter if we don't have God—?
Sunflowers that grow in tenement backyards.
Old men leaning into their own hands. Double Shots of Regret—
The unfinished houses of our lives.

~

When she was gone from there, M wasn't right. I wired him some
    money but I never saw him again.
You are the long blue dress of winter.
You are the light the dead eat at morning.
I am their bowls of teeth, their bellies full of flies. I died long ago
but was reborn and slid back to this place to find you.
I am the window in that church left half open, to let the demons out,
    or in?
The lightning bugs our daughters cup in their hands.
And then he said funeral home. And then he said the beautiful heft of
    your hair.

It was then I wanted to tell him about Desire. But instead I handed
him his ticket at the Greyhound and said what I said.
I hear he is out and so are you and I. So long I am surprised you
    remembered.
I swallowed a tiny yellow pill yesterday and was reminded of it all.

~

How many have come looking for us to find nothing.
Even the whiskey in the room is borrowed.
At the hospital, you tore a hole in the light,
when you climbed out the roof to escape.
We are always escaping, before we were crippled.
I bought you a new pair of flat black shoes.
Heavy as a nun's breasts.
For weddings or funerals? you asked.
And what could I say? Your name lives alone in a small house on
    another occasion.
I did not get an invitation, a card for the annunciation, you
    whispered.
I said, it is an unpublished vacancy, we moved in long ago.
In a country where we do not understand the orders
we would disobey them if we did.
I would grow a beard and you would carry a Molotov cocktail.
Is this what Desire is? Is this the Duende? Then I want to carry a
    machete.
To cut off the wings of the angel.
Look at the blades of your hands, I said. Look at my bleeding
    shoulders.
And then you gasped at my razored wings, peeking out of my gaping
    wounds.

Red Dirt

I went to Brucie's house. I was sixteen.
    Where is your mother, I asked?
Upstairs calling to my aunt, gone for decades.
    We told jokes and poked each other
until we heard his mother in the attic
    softly talking. Then the silence
and the creaking chair from the other side
    of this world.
Red Dirt women can all speak to their dead.

In the Absence of Others I Wanted Something Brave

Yes, I accept I declare to no one. I get on the open road. I remember my father drinking. I'll forget my name except for the ache of my bones. I knew this much was mine. For the poem can call me sweetcakes. Tell me we are out of vegetables. Kiss me full on the mouth. These taboos we try to explain. The data proves it is difficult. Go to the diner: order your sausage and eggs, sup on the slit throats of swine.

Blood-red leaves like knives cut the air of autumn.

Call up the critics, the professors with their funny hats. Ask them what they know about suffering? Their long litanies and references will make the most colicky child fall fast asleep.

What lullaby but the winter wind off the lake, and needing a new coat.

A poem is a wing, a bird without wings. A poem is a sparrow that walks across my snowy lawn this winter, when the wind chill is near 15 below, a poem is a kind of absent song.

A poem is not a bullet, though some may claim. But I imagine a poem could be a bullet. Or is the poem the hole that is left when the bullet goes through?

A poem is not a carburetor. Or a poem could be the carburetor of the human heart. A carburetor that has not been cleaned, a carburetor full of gunk. But I suspect the poem is really written in the scratches in the piston. I suspect the poem is really the gasoline. A poem is a pool of gasoline. Burning.

Sometimes I read these things that say a poem is a theory, or driven by a theory, or written by a certain theory. I see those kinds of poems all the time, some of them have body, climb the ladders of the stair. But is that what a poem is, that makes a poem what we are? The writer bending over to type her theory poem, the hands of another writing his theory poem. All the collisions of empire and class?

I am eating violets. I am pissing on a parked police car outside the Day-Old-Donuts shop. They've named him the Endowed Chair (I mean how funny, how masculine, how drearily obscene). And I imagine the cold wind outside clattering against their tenured walls. They've named their house. They have an Edwardian garden while they declaim they are the Avant-Garde! Viva the Revolution! *As long as our hands remain clean.*

Put down your pen I want to say. Drive out to the edge of town to the State Prison. A poem is the theory of a prisoner. Or the prisoners, bending their backs in their orange jumpsuits, slave labor on the road works. We live in a time where every theory is a failure. We have no need for more literary theories. When cops kill us and the government has slave detention camps up and down the border, and men in dark suits like white hoods make profits.

The poem does not need an award. The poem is for those who've *lost.* The words tenure and poetry should never be in the same sentence. A poem that is almost as translucent as the edge of a slice of apple. The words professor and poetry are at war. For the poem tells the professor, burn the classroom walls to the ground. It tells the professor to plant a tree inside every student's head. And it may bloom, like a revolution.

Follow the lines to the entrance of the gulag. What is it worth, a cup of coffee and a cigarette for a man's life? What is the weight of money when faced with the poem? The poem has dropped out of high school. A poem is not a college, but a collage. A poem is not a university, but a universe. There is nothing to worship like an urn. As soon as one writes it down, the poem changes. It is a spiral, shifting slow above us, a cosmos inside us, like the constellations, like the staircase of our bodies. You can never kill the poem. Erase the poem. The absence of song and the poem is still. There is nothing here about Capital. The poem is the first breath and the last death. It is as hard it is said for a Professor to enter the Kingdom of Poetry as it is for a camel to fit through the 'e' of Helvetica. A poem is not an Academy of Poets. There is no Academy of Poets.

Tamir Rice

I try to translate the Aramaic of the sky.
The violet streaks of dusk

that frame our youngest daughter
drawn in two-point perspective—

she is a you & I, separate
& sublime. Her voice a constant why.

The video she found online, in her head
on repeat. *Why did the policeman shoot the boy?*

she wants to know. *He was playing.*
She climbs into your lap.

Around our daughter's lips, chewed bits
of white petal. She's been eating clover.

The lilac bush scythes
against the wooden fence. In the hive

of the wind, there is something
sickly sweet blowing in.

The swing hangs itself slowly in the dark.

Tattoos

Too often I write "hands" when I mean "sigh." Too often I write "I" when I mean "too few."

~

Too often I've dreamed of Tu Fu, folding his poems into origami boats. He released them into the current to be found down river by peasants who could not read them.

~

The Marx Brothers in *Duck Soup*, "Shhhh, we'll be lost if they find us." "How can we be lost when we are found?"

~

What moment do I have to tell you about the winter today? I walked past the Serbian bar at 7 AM, already saw the old men leaning over their glasses, drinking in the dark.

~

I want to tell you there is a chance for forgiveness. Camus wondered this, as French napalm burned the bodies of Berbers under the North African sun.

~

To decide I am incapable of anything you can ask of any music.

~

To decide instead of a statement, to write: the rain passed over her like a language. The prisoners paused over their shovels together as if deciding the weight of each handful of earth.

~

There was a weight to the wind, it shackled my ankles to the ice. It pushed me down as if praying.

~

The similarity between lovers and readers?

~

Both we are traveling towards—

~

To embrace on the street the stranger for no reason.

~

Other than one was weeping.

Parade Street

November sunlight swooning around the bare tree in my backyard, the crab apples churned to dirt, the gritty sunlight Oppen wrote of—not lemon light— but pale white, a color like chalk the children scribbled across the sidewalk where the boy shot the other boy last week. Alphonso was the dead one's name, who until then I didn't know. His cursive'd name in white and green and blue and brilliant flowers still drawn on the spot where he fell. The other day I saw his little sister I think playing with a crushed can, kicking it by herself down the street. Crushed by the light of November, crushed by the aluminum light: we can climb back into bed, pull the covers over our heads, sing only the dead, as if Alphonso has disappeared, is no more than the bouquet'd requests, the stuffed animals, the handwritten notes, the letters and photos the neighborhood left on the telephone pole where he was shot down. No more than petals, wind-blown, he is breath, breathing as we all are, and the sunlight is breath. And his sister running home now an only child is breath, and there is breathing all up and down Parade Street, past the white boys high on something trying to sell shoplifted toys, or the too-thin girls who lean outside of Pete's Bar calling out to passing cars, and Kay is breath, the elementary school lunch lady sipping a Pabst at the Polish Falcons social club, who tells me how she gave Alphonso *second dessert* at Our Brothers Christian Academy when he was small because even then he was so sweet.

Youngstown Monologue: Captured Light Stained Glass

(after the art by Kimberly Nelson)

This cityscape made of light, each block we live,
each block we bury our dead
who become light,
each square like a coffin,
or are they sheets of granite,
like the ones our fathers
hauled from the quarry,
or the sheets of steel
our fathers unrolled at the mill,
the black smoke & molten ore,
how long since the doors
closed? Oh mother

as you rock in your chair
I see you and your house
hidden in the dark lines,
all those years of shifts
as you drove to Martin
Luther Elementary to serve
lunch in the cafeteria,
now it is all an absence
except when you speak
& the room fills
with the light of stories
of those other children
you loved far from me
that stream through the stained
glass window when I wheel you
to the cathedral on Sunday
to hear another kind of music,
we hear inside our chests,
and each evening when I lift

you out of your wheelchair
and you press against me,
I know to live inside this fragile skin
is to be the light captured by stained glass.

You're Good at Going Under

The lilac bushes shimmer in the evening light, the elms send down their pods of spinning rain. When was the last time that you've eaten? You are good at going under. No one ever sees you weep. Where others shift into survival, a shining place. You dive down deep. To sigh the world its shape, to slip beyond desire into the evidence of everything that seams, you've heard the ringing all around, despite the unclasping of these flowers, the earth opening its outstretched palms as if to plead, the purple loosestrife sprawls along the railroad tracks. You drive down to the lake, the rising of the wind, the dark approaching clouds. There is no slamming of the door. It is a quiet drown. There is never nothing loud.

Far from Any Classroom

far from the talk of writers about writing, far from Harvard, or Yale, or Princeton, far from the bar and the back room at the "writer's conference," far from the book fair, far from the Carnival, where the barkers are selling our lives for a handout, a grant, a bit of good gossip that ruins a career, far from anything named *career*, there in the dives and back streets, there by the carapace of the steel mill in Youngstown, the refinery, the closed-down paper mill along the lake, by the railroad tracks that run to Buffalo and Cleveland and Mumbai, where two girls are blowing up pop cans with M-80s, there in the dust and smoke and their cutoff shorts and their stolen cigarettes, as they walk down the 12th Street tracks towards dusk—there in the sirens and the singed sleeves, there in the basements where someone is putting on a blue dress, unfolding a glow-in-the-dark star chart, where someone can't find their 9 MM, where someone is lacing up their work boots for the last shift at the Forge before they are laid off, and the long drive back through the dark, the small green numbers of the radio bringing a few notes, a few AM psalms. Is all we need, to keep going. Without sorrow is to become something more than sorrow. Never forget. To shape a breath. The chest must rest. Before it rises.

Karaoke Night at the Y Not Bar, Carnegie, PA

She was more beautiful than a stack of empty pallets at the
      end of a night's shift,
this large black woman in a red dress, a slight limp, taking
      the microphone at
the Karaoke bar, the white middle-class accountant type in
      his brown vest
leaning over his pool cue as his opponent, the thick hard
      muscled black man in
a tight white tee and Steelers cap, paused to see this
      woman they must've known
(the joint so small, so sure of itself) open her mouth and
      out came Aretha
Franklin's *I Never Loved a Man the Way I Love You*—she
      took the room apart,
put it back together *better*—her voice's *urgency*

swung a new frying pan upside her man's head, reclaimed
      lost wages, dug
the hard earth, blessed the bar's marriages, mourned its
      miscarriages,
praised the Allegheny mountains
in spring, coal cars uncoupling, unpaid bills burned, thirty
      years of children
and church, Pittsburgh on a Thursday night and no bus fare
      or last call
to the other side of town, long past the hour when the
      mill-gate closed forever
and the second shift spilled out to the Y Not Bar, *Y not sing*
      belted the fat white,
yet blonde and attractive hostess and Sister rose from her
      three sisters (all in their fifties) lining up Long
Island Ice Teas, rose like a slap in the face
      of the ordinary,
to make our little world levitate

enough the meanest foreman
      Saint Michael
might plead, *I'm sorry, have a raise, it's my fault.*

Pittsburgh

Last night I walked, wandered miles through Lawrenceville and Bloomfield, up and around Liberty Ave, past cathedrals and cafeterias, diners named Mama Leona's and boarded houses, heart-shaped graffiti sprayed onto dumpsters, corner bars named Lou's Corner Bar, bookstores where novelists stood behind glass reciting sorrows, a strung-out girl I talked to for a long time named Becky, an old Italian guy named Frankie who said he knew Roberto Clemente, I ate two slices of pizza and gave my crusts to a stray dog. I gave a cigarette to a kid named Juan waiting for the bus, who when I asked what was on his headphones rather than just saying the name recited the lyrics filling the air with unheard verbs. I ended up on a pool table and played so poorly, my friend Cody shaking his head making fragments, I wanted to collage bread, I wanted to collage the steam from a grate with a Pop Warner football game, and a mother in braids yelling, *that's my boy, that's my boy, that's my boy, that's my boy,* like a mantra shouted out against anything. I could have stayed.

Psalm of the Working Poor

It's not that I have nothing.
It's that nothing halves me.

Toledo, Ohio 1977

Fried chicken and sweet potato pie. Blatz beer on our fathers' breath. That autumn Michael and I bagged leaves and burned weed with Anthony, walking house to house with a rake, ringing the doorbell and not running. He taught us how to ask for what we would be owed. We raked and mowed the small lawns of auto parts plant workers and huffed rags from the gas, irrevocably wrecked. Skinny cracker girl Franny, with the racist grandma, bent over algebra equations on her front steps, put them down to dance for us with dark-skinned big-boned Carolyn. They did the Freak to an eight-track disco jam rising out of Mr. Robinson's Lincoln Town Car—doors opened, speakers blaring, he washed that damn car every day. My father sold things, drove long miles, then came home to fall asleep in front of the rabbit ears, my mother off to night school. I sat up late by an AM radio, singing the Isleys, O'Jays, Donny Hathaway's *I've sung a lot of songs, I've made some bad rhymes.* Once Victor's mother the nurse bandaged his hand while smacking him in the head repeatedly for being so stupid, burned by an M-80 he didn't toss fast enough. We were always daring things to explode in our hands. Davey's father's thick arms mapped with scars from the glass factory. Each of his six children wore those scars. And we were all the shards of shiny things, black pieces of coal pressed to diamonds in the pale Ohio light. We were newly shined fenders, carburetors and the grease of a socket wrench. We worshiped ex-ABA rebel ballers, Dr. J rising from the far foul line. We were the color of food stamps and free lunch, blue denim and wide lapels. We were funky as Patti LaBelle chanting, *Voulez-vous coucher avec moi ce soir?* We were missed translations passed hand to hand on tiny slips of paper. We knew the secret signs, read them under a black light. Michael's father, Vietnam vet who sold weed, sat on the back porch, playing his beat-up six-stringed guitar. Oh how he crooned those country tunes dreaming he was Charley Pride. We'd tease his son till he swung an awkward jab then we'd fall down laughing on the cracked sidewalk, scraping our knees. We were Band-Aids ripped off fast. We knew the scars you can't see are the ones that last. Mathew's older brother smuggled us beers out the back door at the UAW hall. We drank them under the bleachers of Scott

High and talked of hoops and high school dances we snuck into and whose bra we lied about undoing, or admired the tough older girls like Franny who slapped us down for getting too close and told us of the places she would go, one day far away as Paris or Marrakesh, or the tenth moon of Jupiter. She smoked her unfiltered cigarettes and stared off at the horizon as the tornado sirens blared. She blew smoke in our faces, tugged on the strap to her halter top. She was doing the math. She already knew the metric system for starlight. The calculus for getting out—

In the Midnight Waking

"Father, why did you work? Why did you weep . . ."
—Louis Simpson

His son died one Saturday night in his sleep. Heart attack at forty-one years. Crazy Larry from my pool team buried his grown son. When Larry called to tell me he couldn't shoot that week, he didn't even tell me his son was dead till I asked if something was wrong. Men are like this, we keep the grief inside unless someone opens a door to let it out. Each word Larry spoke stitched together into a kind of noise I had never before heard. What is difficult to spell, the names of our fathers. The names of our sons. A year later Larry put a bullet in his head. The syllables of guilt and grief we bury in the earth. The sentences that slip through the hallways of the house in the hours after the mourners arrive.

~

Sometimes we are the son, and sometimes we are the father.

~

If a father is a drummer, is the son the skin the father's palms beat upon to make a kind of music?
Or is the father the drum, and the son the sound that rises from its chest?

~

The poet Delmore Schwartz once wrote a poem in the voice of a father:
"You must let me tell you what you fear. *When you wake up from sleep, still drunk with sleep.*"

And in the same poem answered in the voice of the son. *Now I am afraid, what is to be known?*

42

Our fathers quarreling with six pigs. Our fathers shoeing horses, changing oil. Slugging three shots of tequila. Backs bent daily with the bending of labor. Orange coveralls, badges and handcuffs. And then there is our own labor of missing our old man as he's gone to work or county or just absent as sadly so many fathers are: and the others working triple shifts at the plant, this long labor at the plant, working the machines arrhythmic dance, to arrive in this life you must let go a certain form of dream, the long hours coming home covered in grease, a labor like trying to learn a foreign language for perhaps the language of our fathers is always from a foreign country, the blue light burning, as he sat in the car in the driveway for minutes too tired to drive back to work after working a double shift, driving the forklift, working the fryolator, the bureaucrat bent over figures labor, up before his children are awake, asleep when he comes home. How long are the long miles on the road labor, to climb the electric pole to vacuum the floor in a monogram of light, to labor in the ditchlight, bricklight, ashlight, litwick, fistlight, copperlit, light the wick of such human labor, bent backed over trowel or keyboard, warehouses factories and shops and the fluorescent hard light of supermarkets and offices, the labor of not making your quota, of making your quota labor, of a boss who hates you for no reason you can name labor, this labor of loss and grease and going away from the people you love to make money, the labor of what you can't afford to break—

~

If a father is an arrow, who is the bow?

~

My father how he lifted me into the cradle of the tree, how he caught me before I fell, playing catch in a dirt lot along Islington Ave in Toledo, Ohio, or on the basketball court at Fulton School, bending my elbow into a perfect vee and then the follow through. Telling me to look at his brown eyes, his Afro bouncing above his shoulders, and the small rain falling around as we walked home in a late dusk Ohio evening covered in sweat. I think of him as I watch this young black father on the lawn of Central Tech, as I waited at the light. He was wearing a Steelers shirt and threw a football in a long spiral, calling out plays to his tall skinny son running in long red Nike shorts, topless and wiry in the humid late summer dusk, his old man bending to tussle the hair of his son, who hiked the ball as his father called out *run son run son run run run*

~

Are we always running away from our fathers?

~

Are we always running back into the arms of our fathers?

~

What do we catch from our fathers? What talk must some of our fathers tell us to save our lives?

~

If the father is the bow, is the son the arrow?

~

If the son is an arrow, is the father the bow?

~

I never see my son, he has turned seventeen. My son is tall as tasseled corn in late summer. He is sweet but cocksure, all elbows and knees. He is out in the underground smoky places where he runs, in the basements pasted with fliers and posters where the punk bands push the bodies of boys into collisions with bass lines and brash guitars. He is tall and lean and getting some of the razor I have longed to grow inside his sweet demeanor for the world we live in is a place of cruel and often unforgiving formalities and institutions. He calls me less. His tone grown curt. I want to hug him and smack him at the same time more often than not, that sarcastic teenage tone that makes me cringe, this tall thin curly-headed stranger who smells like a man not like the child I'd stay up late to rock and wipe his fevered head. But there is also something there so far beyond me it is like looking at a distant cloud, or that feeling when the geese begin to cover the sky in vees. He is leaving me and I am feeling something mixed inside the bowl of the second O of sorrow. An ancient soup of passage that perhaps every father has supped since the first spear was thrown above the tall grass of the Serengeti. He lives on the other side of town with his mother. She says to me, these days I don't know too often what is going on inside him. Does he speak to you? I want to tell her, *he shares everything with me*, but what would that lie do? So instead I tell the truth. *I get a few words*, I tell her, and think like the few words she and I were reduced to by the end of us years ago. Now we chat easy of this strange man-boy we share like when we were young and still believed we would go on together, and the worry we pass back and forth like a report card, or a gift we don't know how to accept. What I do not tell her is when I miss him, when he is out late or distant, it isn't just him this tall stranger that I miss and worry so about, it is that three-year-old who woke from a thunderstorm or from a bad dream and frightened came running down the hallway and climbed into our bed.

Our sons we never stop seeing them as when we carried them to sleep.

~

At evening slumped in his chair after work. After the long hours on the road, my father came home to our red brick tenement flat and drank and talked. My father could really drink, but he was even better at talking. He had a history degree. He'd pour the Bacardi and tell me about Alexander Nevsky, or the Wobblies, or Nat Turner or the Molly Maguires. He knew all the great battles and what and who made the revolutions. He once wanted to be a teacher but took whatever job he found selling things to feed us. The same as so many fathers—the factory smell of someone's father's hands. He taught you how to tie your shoes by tying his work boots. The palm calluses on his roughened palms. The smell of aftershave and diesel.

My father talked and talked but I did not listen. What did I know then? Some dumb kid worried about my girlfriend or getting high? What would I give to go back to those years and eavesdrop on his monologue?

O father a thousand miles away, I am now older than you were when I left that flat along the red brick rows and never went back.

~

If the father is the reel, is the son the line? Squatting on white buckets side by side along the pier? Or is the son the lure the father casts into the lake, and never despite everything reels back in?

~

If the son is an arrow, when does the father let him fly?

~

If the father is a bow, is the son the arrow?

Or maybe the son is the bow, and shoots the arrow
straight into the target of his father's chest?
Tonight the whole world is a house with one light burning.

~

Come home, son, I say, come home to your father,
lay your weary head on this shoulder
and let me smell your hair for I am old,
then help me down from this tree
as when I held you up,
lifting your bloody just-born body
up before the Sun, O son, O Holy holy son.

Leaking Light

This malingering influenza running along the lake. Perhaps this is how we will all go, slowly, one cough at a time, the way the last century slid away, with one quiet turn of the earth. I guess if we are not gunned down that is how we go anyways, the most of us, slowly, and then one day one of us isn't here, then another. Joe Rash had a heart attack. Doc finally walked into that good light. Larry shot himself. Frenchy just stopped breathing of old age. One day he was there playing billiards and cracking jokes right beside me, such a graceful old man. All the old pool players passing on, leaving behind their ghosts. Sometimes I forget and wonder maybe Joe will be in and bank a few with me, his slight shuffle, his gentle and deft dark hands. He held the cue lightly on his fingertips like reading Braille. He let the cue ball fly. I shout at some wise-ass kid asking for a table, no you can't have table 20, Frenchy will be in soon. I forget he isn't coming. Frenchy who was over 80, fought in Korea, who between games shot his insulin, the small prick and bleed. Lined up his pills. His wiry wisp of white hair. His glasses thick as stained glass. He was always leaking light. His voice deep as any river. He's fading though, they are all fading, fast as the rain rushing over the great lake, sometimes I see them out there, flying like kites, these men, my gone friends: drawn windblown across the felt of the sky in blue chalk.

My Youngest Daughter Brings Me Daisies and Bits of Plastic Trash

A long hazy day we climb the air as if a ladder. The black branches of the lilac have blossomed overnight. My neighbor is outside watering her crocuses, wearing the cheap accoutrements of Annunciation, a blue Greek rosary dangling like a necklace from her neck. The first hot wind is carrying something close to faith, or at least the promise of faith. My daughter is digging in the dirt. She brings me daisies. She brings me bits of plastic trash. She names them rubies. She names them "star litter." My neighbor is slightly drunk and walks as if she has wings, like a ballet dancer up on her toes. My daughter walked like this her first few years, the thing that told her therapist she has the palsy. She tiptoed around the house her arms gangling and flapping with joy. I named her my furious bird. We named her Akhmatova (the dark light we made her out of), waiting at the gates, like our neighbor who I am realizing is extraordinarily intoxicated, she is starting to slur and sing. My daughter now is climbing a staircase of light. The steaming laundry of the air. The trees are full of crows and grackles. I praise her body leaping vespers. She moves irregular as a votive candle's flame. What can be strung together, these moments, are made of love, the dusk writes itself across her face. The electrocardiogram of sky above the trees is where she's headed. Now she runs her fast and awkward gait across the lawn, her furious lisped-and-spittle speech. Her hands are sparrows. Her hands are poems.

Biography of LeBron as Ohio

When is a poem one word? Even at 17 he was Baraka
     on the court, Coltrane gold toned, a kind of running riff,
more than boy-child, man-child, he was one word like Prince.
     How back in those drunken days when I still
ran in bars & played schoolyard ball
     & wagered fives & tens, me & my colleague
the pysch-prof drove across Eastern Ohio
     just to see this kid from powerhouse St. Vincent,
grown out of rust-belt-bent-rims, tripped
     with the hype & hope & hip hop
blaring from his headphones, all rubber soled
     & grit as the city which birthed him.
We watched him rise that night scoring over 35,
     drove back across the quiet cut cornfields
& small towns of Ohio, back to the places
     where we slept knowing that Jesus had been reborn, black
& beautiful with a sweatband crown rimming his brow.
     He was so much more than flipping burgers & fries,
more than 12-hour shifts at the steel plant in Cleveland.
     More than the shut-down mill in Youngstown.
More than that kid selling meth in Ashtabula.
     He was every kid, every street, every silo, he was white
& black & brown & migrant kids working farms.
     He was the prince of stutter-step & pause. He was the new
King. We knew he was coming back the day after he left
     his house in Bath Township. He never sold it.
Someone fed his fish for years. Perhaps our hope? Fuck Miami.
Leave Wade to wade through the Hurricane rain. LeBron is
remembering that woman washing the linoleum floor, that man
     punching his punch card. He drives a Camaro, the cool kid
Ohio car driving through any Main Street. He is the toll-taker, &
     he is the ticket out.
He keeps index cards documenting
     his opponents' moves. One leans forward before he drives.
One always swipes with his left hand. The details like a preacher

studying the gospel. He studies the game like a
mathematician conjugating equations, but when he moves he is a
        choreography,
a conductor passing the ball like a baton. He is a burst of cinders
        at the mill. He is a chorus of children calling his name.
        The blistered hands of a man stacking boxes
in Sandusky, the long wait for work in Lorain.
A sapling bends
        & reaches in all directions
before it becomes a tree. A ball is a key to a lock.
        A ball is the opposite of Glock.
America who sings your praises,
        while tying the rope, everyone waiting for Caesar to fall,
back-stabbing media hype city betrayed
        by white people with racist signs.
        I watch the kids play ball
in the Heights, witness this they say. We will rise. I watched
        LeBron arrive & leave, I walked, I gave up drinking
as he went off & won a ring. The children's chorus calls out sing
        brother, sing. Everything is black. Storm clouds gather
out on Lake Erie. But the old flower-hatted women
        at the Baptist church are handing out praise cards,
registering teenagers to vote. To turn a few words into a sentence.
He is a glossary of jam, & yes he is corporate
        chugging down green bubbly Sprite, running in Beats head
phones, he is Dunkin his donut, he is Nike, witness, ripped.
        On a spring day in Akron a
chorus of children is chanting his name on the court by the
chain-link fence. He is forged steel, turning his skinny body into
        muscle, years of nights lifting, chiseling, cutting, studying.
Watching the tape. To make a new kind of sentence. He is passing
        out T-shirts, this long hot bloody summer he was returned
to the rusted rim along the big lake. He is stutter-step. He is
        spinning wheel. He has a cool new hat. He is speaking of dead
black children. He is giving his time. To make the crowd
        sway like wind through a field of corn.
        Does LeBron think of dying?
        Does the grape think of dying as it withers on the vine by

the lake? Or does it dream of the wine it will become?
He is wearing a shirt that says I Can't Breathe.
They said he was arrogant. I said he was just Ohio.

      He married his high school sweetheart. Bravado laid out
on the court. No back down, he is Biggie with a basketball inside
      of a mic, no ballistics, just ballet. He is Miles Davis cool,
quietly cerebral, turning his back, tossing up
      chalk like blue smoke, blue notes, blues. He is Akron,
Columbus, he is heart & Heat turned to lake effect blizzards,
      freighters frozen in ice, looking for work & no money to eat.
He is Ashtabula & Toledo. He is carrying so many across the
      river, up through Marietta.
      The grapevines are ripe in Geneva.
      He returns, Man-child, Man-strong, Man-smart, Man-
mountain, Mansfield to East Akron, minus into Man, or should we
      say Mamma raised? Single mother fed, shy child, quiet child,
who grew, who suffered & taught his body to sing, his
      mother worked how many shifts, doing this, doing that,
never gave up for her son. He is third shift at the rubber
      plant in winter, he is farm hands & auto parts piecework
& long nights the men at the bar, eyes on the television.
      The lake tonight is black as newly laid asphalt.
There are no ellipses. He is turning paragraphs
      into chapters. Long ago the hoop Gods made this deal
at the crossroads, Old Scratch is flipping the pages
      of his program & waiting high in the stands—to belong to a
place most people would call
      nowhere, to show the world how tough we truly are,
twelve-hour shifts at the Rubber plant in Akron. How he is, how
      he is a part of this asphalt court we call Ohio, & how we
suffer, & how we shine.

Poem Made of East Sides

I trace the stitching of clouds in the blue sheet of sky stretching above
the long slab of our lives, this autopsy I start with words, toe
tagging the people we were.

Zip guns and the zigzag clothesline across the East Side sky. Your
grandfather riding his bike, humming in Polish, Kishka and a loaf
of bread in a bag. Before and after the wars, we are always riding
our bikes in the rain.

The only light we have in our lives is the light from broken glass.

Nothing that is whole is art.

That woman I passed waiting in the rain, in her Wendy's uniform,
sitting on an overturned shopping cart someone had wheeled from
the Plaza, tired of standing one time too many waiting for the bus.

Scoring in the Safeway parking lot.

The tight noose along the arm, the pockmarked wrists. Michele, you
haunt me lately,

30 years ago, in an East Side three flight tenement (we used to walk up
three flights of outside stairs to get to your room, to get to how
many rooms? We didn't question anything back then.)

"I think of my mother, the chemo, the endless tests, her pocked arm."

The difference is when I see a hypodermic I don't see my childhood

doctor, the visit, the memory of first shots, I see my dead.

I walked by a doorway in Cleveland Heights, an addict or runaway or
both, a girl with a nose-ring, the wisp of her thick eyebrows, her
dirty dreadlocked white-girl hair, with the face of someone

I used to hold, a name I uttered softly as the rain falling on both our
heads.

The shine of a stranger's hand as she reaches towards me.

The bruises on our elbows and shins.

We are two lanterns burning our own inexhaustible oils.

We are the outstretched autobiography of our razored limbs.

Elegy on the Side of a Milk Carton

The seamstress disappeared,
who walked along the road, in her absence
a space, like the indent in a bed. Can you hear
her sewing the bar smoke, sewing the rain
into a pall, sewing the incense
from the priest's thurible, or the hands that held
her shoulders down? And after they were done
with her, she took like black thread her long hair
and stitched closed the hole she'd torn in the air—

Eating Sea Roses in the Afterlife

When we argued it was like I was throwing oranges at you. You bit the rind of each word with your teeth. In the CITGO parking lot we saw the meteor shower and felt scrubbed by a celestial light. You wore that Canadian army jacket you stole from Salvation Army. Your eyes were overflowing with bicycles. Somehow even though I couldn't understand a word you were saying you weren't making sense you were—kissing you was like eating Lucky Charms and watching cartoons on a rainy Saturday. Tell me a story you said: *somehow, I feel I am always that boy jumping off the bridge; so cheap this life we couldn't even count its change.* We never shared our food but we tasted everything. I saved salt packages for you in the cup holder of the car. And then there were the bandages, and the doctors. Listening to the wounded rain. We fucked like snarling wolves. I swallowed all of the pills you gave me. They were yellow the color of urine analysis. We lived in a house of strays. There was a dove who sang in the willow tree. You handed me the black bough. You were endlessly I suppose each time all gone. When what you loved you said was more than the far-off fireworks. On the fourth of July. We set the roof, the roof of the house accidentally on fire.

Down the Line

Johnny Cash is playing on repeat on the jukebox. No one here drinks
drinks named after birds. Bill from the West Side Biker Gang is arm
wrestling this huge Dominican dude I nicknamed one brave drunk
night El Tiante. They are laughing as they call each other *motherfucker*.
Motherfucker is everybody's middle name here. *Got to move on down the
line.* Don't even try to figure it out. The smoke curls like eyelashes.
The light is nearly violet. The felt on the pool table is always ripped.
Outside the street is full of booms from fireworks, the night sky
plumage like a peacock's tail. I'm watching Harry, who did two tours
in Iraq; he seems jittery, bending his chin down to his drink, then
squinting and rocking with himself at the bar. Leaning into the two-
fisted shots of Jack. It is over 80 proof in here & sweat pours out
of the yellow papered walls, with its stains shaped like the maps of
countries named Stan. *Gotta move on down the line.* The Puerto Rican
bikers are playing darts & calling each other *Puta*. Ralphie, in his red
leather chaps, is leaning some woman with tall gold hair against the
wall. Their mouths melt like votive candles. And someone suddenly
opens the steel door and the outside pops in—BAM BAM BAM, &
half of us not drunk enough to know better duck. But it's just a bunch
of white kids tossing M-80s into the metal garbage can. The night
is a chorus of sound, some intimate & some strange & unfamiliar as
some faraway country we left behind in another lifetime, the thatched
villages of our fathers & our dead. Vlad the Slav is on his 12th round.
He's mouthing lyrics to *Down the Line*, when he stands up straight as
a statue of Tito, lifts his shot glass of vodka, and roars *Gonna get what
chu ain't got, she'll be sweet and won't do me wrong.* And then the jukebox and
everyone shouts back as if they know the only words that might save
us, *She'll be cool and twice as gone—*

Our Love as Lead Belly or

What howling, what teeth pick
& guitar, chords
to slash across our limbs
against their lynch mobs,

howling what
homicide, love shack
south bound steel
train, fallen
caribou, rip the flesh
& feed the blind & yelping
tongues, in smoky lounge
this skin, we open
our bodies & shed
this myth, finger
the frets of our necks,
in the dark den, hackles
raised, naked
& discordant
we wake, like a broken
xylophone, mixed up
conjoined skeletons.
Praise our gnawed bones.

You Are Beautiful as the Absence of the Air

You are beautiful as a dialect of glass, as the longest slide in a little girl's dream. *I'm Nobody,* but you are conch shells and haikus: asleep you become / marshland full of nesting birds / at light you are songs. Beautiful as the Metropolitan Opera singing *Aida,* as a full grocery cart, pushed in the hands of the old lady with the green scarf at the Kroger's, who I gave my EBT card. As the biggest pot of collards, as punching out on the factory clock, as a kennel full of sleeping Siberian Husky pups, you are full-throated dark-knowing, beautiful as scarved women, suddenly rising from the picket line outside of the gated mill, on the last day of the strike. As Portuguese madrigals sung in a far-off cathedral, as painkillers and cigarette-stained hands, on the counter of the last bar open in town, and the neon casting azure shadows on the parking lot gravel, when I am waiting to take you home after working a long shift, you are as beautiful as the stone our daughter finds, on the beach, which is we see a piece of glass, worn tear-shaped and ruby red, you are beautiful as Miles Davis pouring through *Bitches Brew,* as the intricate threads woven by monks in a medieval tapestry at The Cloisters, as women in their black netted wailing along the ditches, as the joy of my dead grandfather opening up a can of sardines or a grinning face scripted in coal dust on a window by a child's finger, down at the bus station where we waited in West Virginia, remember the freshly fallen snow covered with our daughter's imprint as she lay down making angels, she is a grammar without translation. You are beautiful as any gerund unattended, my random winning lottery number drawn.

Rain, Gas, Boone County, West Virginia,

There is only a roof & one pump
There is only the dark road
There is only the grocer Mel
I hear a man ask Mel
I'll take that can of Longhorn
& his shelves of dusty cans
Chiclets & RC Cola
Jerky & yellow-edged maps
There is only a key
That someone turns in the sky
To open it & let the dark pour down
The mountains are smoldering
With machines
Bearded men are buying cigarettes
I pump my gas in the absence of light
On a road that belongs to dead men
I will drive toward nothing straight
I hand the cashier
A packet of jerky & ask for a pack of Camels
I wish I could say more
I wish I could tell you about the gun
I wish I was more than a body
That I was growing that my collarbones
Were not hollow
As my grandfather's before he died
This man has duct tape on his work boot
The kind of rip says you lost a toe
And I recall the dust of the newspaper plant
Used to turn to shimmering gold flecks
When we'd work the night shift to dawn
The light pouring in around the machines
The silence
Of sleeping houses
Far from the road
I can almost hear

The snoring of strangers
I do not need directions
Since I am headed nowhere
My mother would say my hair is unkempt
I haven't changed in days
How our lives are rewritten
Until they say nothing
That matters
More than leaving
As a story is anyone
We all have a beginning & an end
The men surprise me as I turn
Good luck young fella
And go on talking about some kind
Of accident high up the mountain
In this world where a man's life
Is worth less than the weight of anthracite
I try to forget the load I carry
Is what can't be left behind
I drive through the rain's wreckage
Despite the evidence my headlights
Open a door in the dark.

Gertrude Stein Lighthouse Sonnet

To kiss darkly in the dark park's
parking lot is to kiss the dark

sparks leaping from our lighthouse lips
along the great lake's cliffs,

warning the night boats
casting their dark lures,

down to where even the light
does not reach, where the bones

of ancient freighters rest
below the giant bass

whose great mouths O
as they pull against the glint

of the hook, and rise grand
and glistening on the barbs of moonlight

DJ Jehovah

My daughter & I keep digging in the dirt even after it starts to drizzle.
I am planting onions & basil, oregano & parsley. The tomato plants
stand potted, the rain falls on our house, on our neighbor's house,
my friends Carlos & Hector the ones with the plumbing business
who drink Tequila at night & get into loud shouting matches about
soccer games they watch on cable, hitting the patio table & cursing
out loud in the wire fenced backyard two houses down. If they got
together with my Bosnian neighbor Samir, who likes to drink vodka
and shout at his uncles, who likes to kick a soccer ball against our
fence, roasting the lamb, they'd realize the only difference in the
world is their words, not what they say, some version of *jebi si* (go fuck
yourself) and *que chingados* (what the fuck!). But this weekday they are
at work. The neighborhood is quiet except for the faraway rumble of
the 12th Street train, me and Akhmatova, my three-year-old black-
gated daughter, are digging into the earth. It is what we do. We dig.
Her mother is in the house trying to rest, her bandaged foot, the
relentless pain. She needs to sleep. She takes a pill, she pours a drink.
She passes out. What else can one do? It is May. The crocuses have
long bloomed. Everything has opened. The air is white with wisteria.
Our daughter reaches up to eat the drizzle. She is done digging.
The rain is falling harder now, yet we stay out in the downpour,
it is washing us to the bone, my shirt hangs heavy as a nun's habit.
My daughter's knees once black & smeared with dirt are clean. Her
hair pressed down flat against her riveted face. Our daughter runs
splashing in circles, she runs with a palsy limp, she picks & eats the
tiny white petals of the wild strawberries growing along the chain-
link fence. Can you see her? The rain it falls like melted wax. We
are no spectacle. No document to say we lived. We are a rough &
ordinary music. The DJ in the clouds turns the records of our lives.
My daughter & I, arms outstretched, spin like two turntables.

Something Lovely as the Rain

When pain pauses a new world emerges, something lovely as the rain, or like the sunlight strolling in the afternoon without teeth. Or a cracked egg, or a piece of glass. The wind blew your long lashes. And what was fear left hanging, or tossed on the waves. Or should I say bay, we walked beside. The cottonwood was floating. Children flew kites. The schools were closed down. The kites you said, are like lilies on fragile strings. You did not say butterflies. Though the monarchs were fluttering on the milkweed. Despite the heat, your scarred hands were blue crosses. You were not in a wheelchair, we limped slowly along. Every now and then someone would fall on roller skates. What if we ate the wild roses, you said, petal by petal, disarming the silence, the sense that something would happen? Where were our daughters? Even this already seemed like a story. Did I mention we were poor, except for a bag of almonds I stole from the corner store? There was something nearing music, the locusts were whirring. Birds in the sky like Chinese brushstrokes. And you were blooming into nothing that could stay—

Grief's Familiar Rooms

Sometimes I am okay
even though when I come home

from work,
I still sit in your chair for hours

without taking my coat off
pulling at its buttons

that are not answers—

Acknowledgments

Blessings to the editors of the following journals for their support of these poems, sometimes in different versions, genres, or with different titles:

2 Bridges Review: "Tattoos";

Birmingham Poetry Review: "My Youngest Daughter Brings Me Daisies and Bits of Plastic Trash";

Blue Earth Review: "In the Midnight Waking";

BOAAT: "Down the Line";

Brevity: "Toledo, Ohio 1977";

The Collagist: "The Second O of Sorrow," "Portrait Written with a Cough";

Congeries: "Pittsburgh," "The Bravery of Birds";

Crab Creek Review: "Scribbled on the Scaffolding of";

Descant: "Youngstown Monologue: Captured Light Stained Glass," "You Are Beautiful as the Absence of the Air";

Diode: "My Grief Grows a White Flower," "Grief," "Grief's Familiar Rooms";

Flagler Review: "Gertrude Stein Lighthouse Sonnet";

Forklift: "Triptych of Desire and the Duende";

Glass Poetry Journal: "Far from Any Classroom";

H_ngm_n: "We Pay the Rent We Breathe";

The Healing Muse: "Something Lovely as the Rain";

Laurel Review: "What Do You Say To a Daughter When She Suspects Her Mother Is Dying";

Matter: "Poem Made of East Sides";

Moon City Review: "Psalm of the Working Poor";

Ninth Letter (Online Special Midwest Writers Issue): "Biography of LeBron as Ohio";

North American Review: "DJ Jehovah";

Poetry East: "Karaoke at the Y Not Bar, Carnegie, PA";

Radar: "You're Good at Going Under";

Stone Canoe: "Elegy on the Side of a Milk Carton," "We a New Ledger";

Talking River Review: "Leaking Light," "Our Love as Lead Belly or"; *Upstreet*: "Parade Street."

"You are Beautiful as the Absence of the Air" received the 2015 Betsy Colquitt Poetry Award from Texas Christian University's *Descant Literary Review*.

"In the Absence of Others I Wanted Something Brave" was published in the anthology *Manifesto* (University of Akron Press, 2016), edited by Alan Michael Parker and Rebecca Hazelton.

These poems would not exist without the support and bravery against the odds of my partner, Lisa Akus, and my children: my son Gabriel, and my daughters Amara Rumi, and Andaluzja Akhmatova.

Sources for the epigrams: January Gill O'Neil from her poem "Questions of Sleep" published in her book *Misery Island* (CavanKerry Press, 2014). Land of Talk (Elizabeth Powell) from the song "Some Are Lakes" off the album *Land of Talk* (Saddle Creek Records, 2008); John T. Irwin's book, *Apollinaire lived in Paris, I Live in Cleveland, Ohio,* (John Hopkins University Press, 2011); Susan Aizenberg from her poem "Art" published in her book *Muse* (Southern Illinois University Press, 2002).

Gratitude and love to my editor and publisher Peter Conners and everyone at BOA for all you do for poetry.

Thank you to Poet's Hall, Civitas, and Mercyhurst University for bestowing upon me a Lifetime Achievement Award for Poetic Achievement.

Thank you Cee, Greg, Christina, and to the Erie poetry and pool communities particularly, Bigg Wash, Matt and Marc Borczon, Monica Igras, Kat, Chuck, Kim, Tom and Daren.

Gratitude to these fine people who offered encouragement, support friendship or inspiration during the writing of these poems: Jeffrey McDaniel, Kevin Goodan, Kimberly Burwick, Luisa A. Igloria,

Patrick Rosal, Julie Babcock, Jose Padua, Ernesto Mercer, Phil Metres, Sheryl St. Germain, Roger Bonair-Agard, Joel Dias Porter, Al Maginnes, Maria Gillan, Martin Espada, Carolyn Forche, Lee Upton, Ra Washington, Oliver De La Paz, Robert Fanning, Dorianne Laux, Justin Lightfoot Bigos, Brian Gilmore, Silvana Straw, Karen Craigo, Les Kay, Derek McKown, Cheryl Dumesnil, Liz Ahl, Holly Wendt, Laura Moran, Gloria Mindock, Jeremy Shraffenburger, Vince Gotera, Rachel Morgan, Jim O'Laughlin, Les Roka, Christian Anton Gerard, Micah Towery, Matthew Olzmann, Sarah Shotland, Adam Love, Ray McManus, Jeffrey Thompson, George Guida, Jennifer Sweeny, Chad Sweeny, Jessica Lizardi, William Stobb, Barbara Unger, Jason Baldinger, Karen Schubert, Reginald Dwayne Betts, John Hoppenthaler, M.L. Liebler, BJ Ward, John Smith, Joe Weil, Emily Vogel, Laure-Anne Bosselaar, Steve Kuusisto, Sarah Freligh, Albert Abonado, Phil Memmer, Cary Waterman, Sass Brown, Alicia Mathias, Patrick Werle, John Gallaher, Chad Burrall, Lisa Fay Coutley, Tony Vallone, Marc Jacksina, Tacoma White, Scott Beal, Tim Suermondt, Terry Blackhawk, Alex Lemon, Martha Silano, Barbara Jane Reyes, Meg Kearney, Erika Meitner, Susan Blackwell Ramsey, and the late and dearly missed: Cody Todd, Derick Burleson, and June King.

Notes:
On November 24, 2014, twelve-year-old Tamir Rice was murdered in broad daylight at Cudell Recreation Center in Cleveland, Ohio, by Cleveland rookie patrolman Timothy Loehmann. Rice had been playing with an air soft gun when Loehmann, in response to a 911 call that said the gun may be a toy, pulled up, opened the door and shot Rice. Video evidence showed Loehmann pulled his gun in two seconds. After the shooting, he and his partner Frank Garmback did not attempt any first aid on Tamir, who died later that day at the hospital. No charges were filed against either officer.

The title for "In the Midnight Waking" was taken from the poem "Come Up from the Fields Father" by Walt Whitman.

About the Author

Sean Thomas Dougherty has worked in a newspaper plant, as a security guard, a poet in the schools, a teacher of parolees, as an untenured college lecturer, in a pool hall, as a caregiver and medical technician for people with traumatic brain injuries, and as a performer. For over thirty years he has also been a writer. He is the author or editor of fifteen books, including *All You Ask for Is Longing: Poems 1994–2014, Sasha Sings the Laundry on the Line*; and *Broken Hallelujahs*, all published by BOA Editions. His awards include a Fulbright Lectureship to the Balkans, and an appearance in *The Best American Poetry*. He lives in Erie, Pennsylvania, with the poet Lisa Akus and their two daughters, Amara Rumi and Andaluzja Akhmatova.

BOA Editions, Ltd.,
American Poets Continuum Series

Colophon

BOA Editions, Ltd., a not-for-profit publisher of poetry and other literary works, fosters readership and appreciation of contemporary literature. By identifying, cultivating, and publishing both new and established poets and selecting authors of unique literary talent, BOA brings high-quality literature to the public. Support for this effort comes from the sale of its publications, grant funding, and private donations.

The publication of this book is made possible, in part, by the support of the following individuals:

Anonymous
Jan & Ken Bailey
Angela Bonazinga & Catherine Lewis
Chris & DeAnna Cebula
Art & Pam Hatton
Grant Holcomb
Jack & Gail Langerak
Peter Makuck
Melanie & Ron Martin-Dent
Joe McElveney
Boo Poulin
Deborah Ronnen & Sherman Levey
Steven O. Russell & Phyllis Rifkin-Russell
Lee Upton, *in memory of Lana Upton*
Michael Waters & Mihaela Moscaliuc